WOODLAND
WILDLIFE
T0061195
North American
Black Bears
by G. G. Lake
CAPSTONE PRESS
a capstone imprint
Pebble
Plus

Pebble Plus is published by Capstone Press,
1710 Roe Crest Drive, North Mankato, Minnesota 56003
www.mycapstone.com

Copyright © 2017 by Capstone Press, a Capstone imprint. All rights reserved.
No part of this publication may be reproduced in whole or in part, or stored in a retrieval system, or transmitted in any form or by any means, electronic, mechanical, photocopying, recording, or otherwise, without written permission of the publisher.

Library of Congress Cataloging-in-Publication Data
Names: Lake, G. G., author.
Title: North American Black bears / by G. G. Lake.
Description: North Mankato, Minnesota : Capstone Press, [2017] | Series: Pebble plus. Woodland wildlife | Audience: Ages 4–8 | Audience: K to grade 3 | Includes bibliographical references and index.
Identifiers: LCCN 2016001920| ISBN 9781515708148 (library binding) | ISBN 9781515708216 (pbk.) | ISBN 9781515708278 (ebook (pdf))
Subjects: LCSH: Black bear—Juvenile literature.
Classification: LCC QL737.C27 L3275 2017 | DDC 599.78/5—dc23
LC record available at http://lccn.loc.gov/2016001920

Editorial Credits
Gena Chester, editor; Juliette Peters, designer;
Wanda Winch, media researcher; Steve Walker, production specialist

Photo Credits
Corbis: Design Pics/Michael DeYoung, 17; iStockphoto: Dieter Meyri, 19; Shutterstock: alicedaniel, illustrated forest items, Anna Subbotina, 22–23, AR Pictures, tree bark design, Critterbiz, cover, 5, 13, elina, 24, Ian Maton, 9, jadimages, 21, mythja, 1, Stawek, 11 (map), Sunny Forest, 3; Thinkstock: Bjorn Bakstad, 11 (top), Capturing_Essence, 7, Frank Hildebrand, 15; Visuals Unlimited, Tom Ulrich, 12

Note to Parents and Teachers

The Woodland Wildlife set supports national curriculum standards for science related to life science. This book describes and illustrates North American black bears. The images support early readers in understanding the text. The repetition of words and phrases helps early readers learn new words. This book also introduces early readers to subject-specific vocabulary words, which are defined in the Glossary section. Early readers may need assistance to read some words and to use the Table of Contents, Glossary, Read More, Internet Sites, Critical Thinking Using the Common Core, and Index sections of the book.

Printed in the United States 5139

Table of Contents

Clawed Climbers 4
Forest Homes 10
Finding Food. 14
Life Cycle 18

Glossary. 22
Read More 23
Internet Sites 23
Critical Thinking
Using the Common Core . 24
Index 24

Clawed Climbers

A big black animal climbs
up a tree. His curved claws
and big paws help him climb fast.
He's a North American black bear!

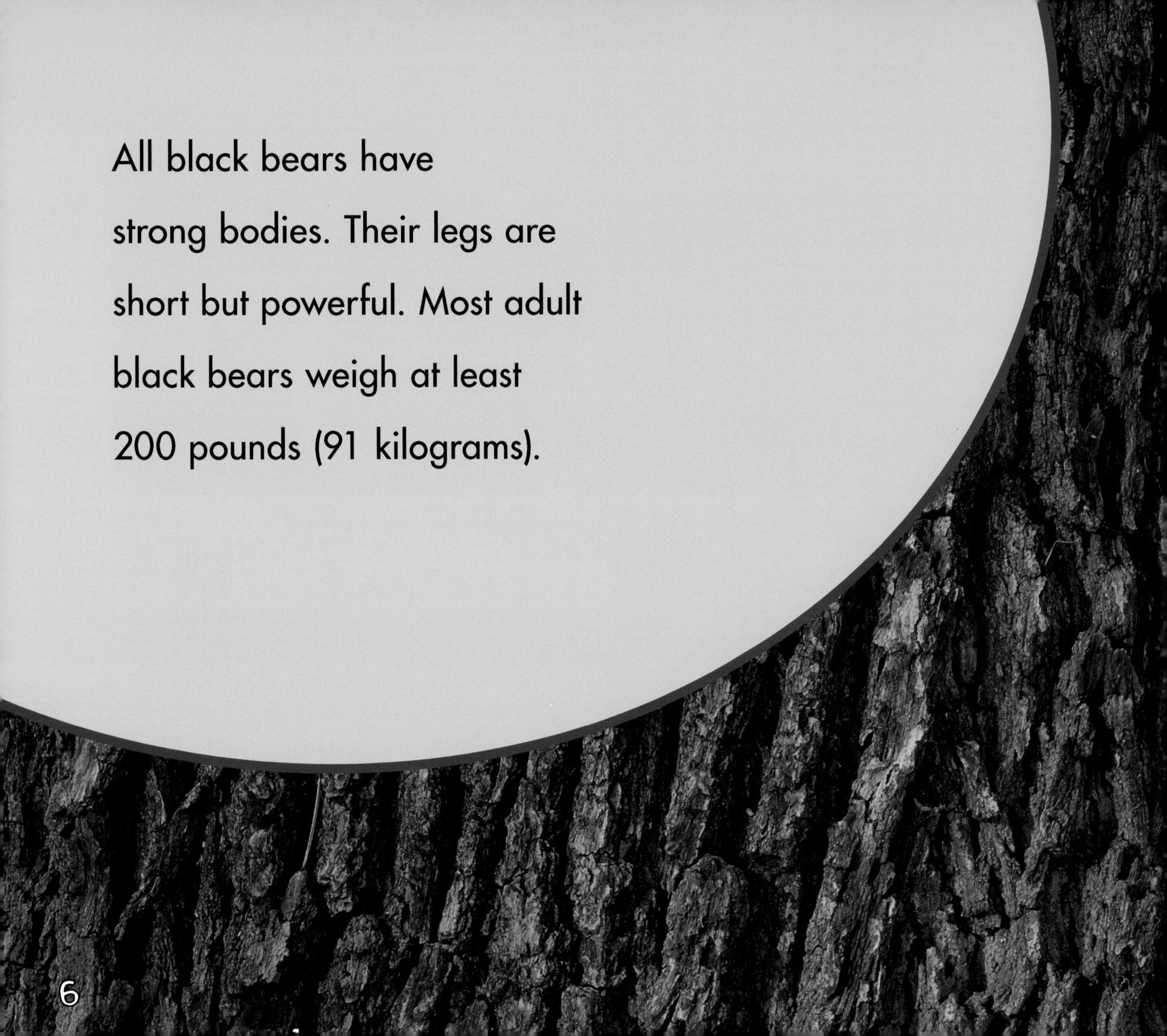

All black bears have strong bodies. Their legs are short but powerful. Most adult black bears weigh at least 200 pounds (91 kilograms).

Black bears do not always have black fur. Their fur can be black or brown. Black bears have lighter fur around their muzzles.

muzzle

Forest Homes

Black bears are found throughout North America. They live in the woods and near water.

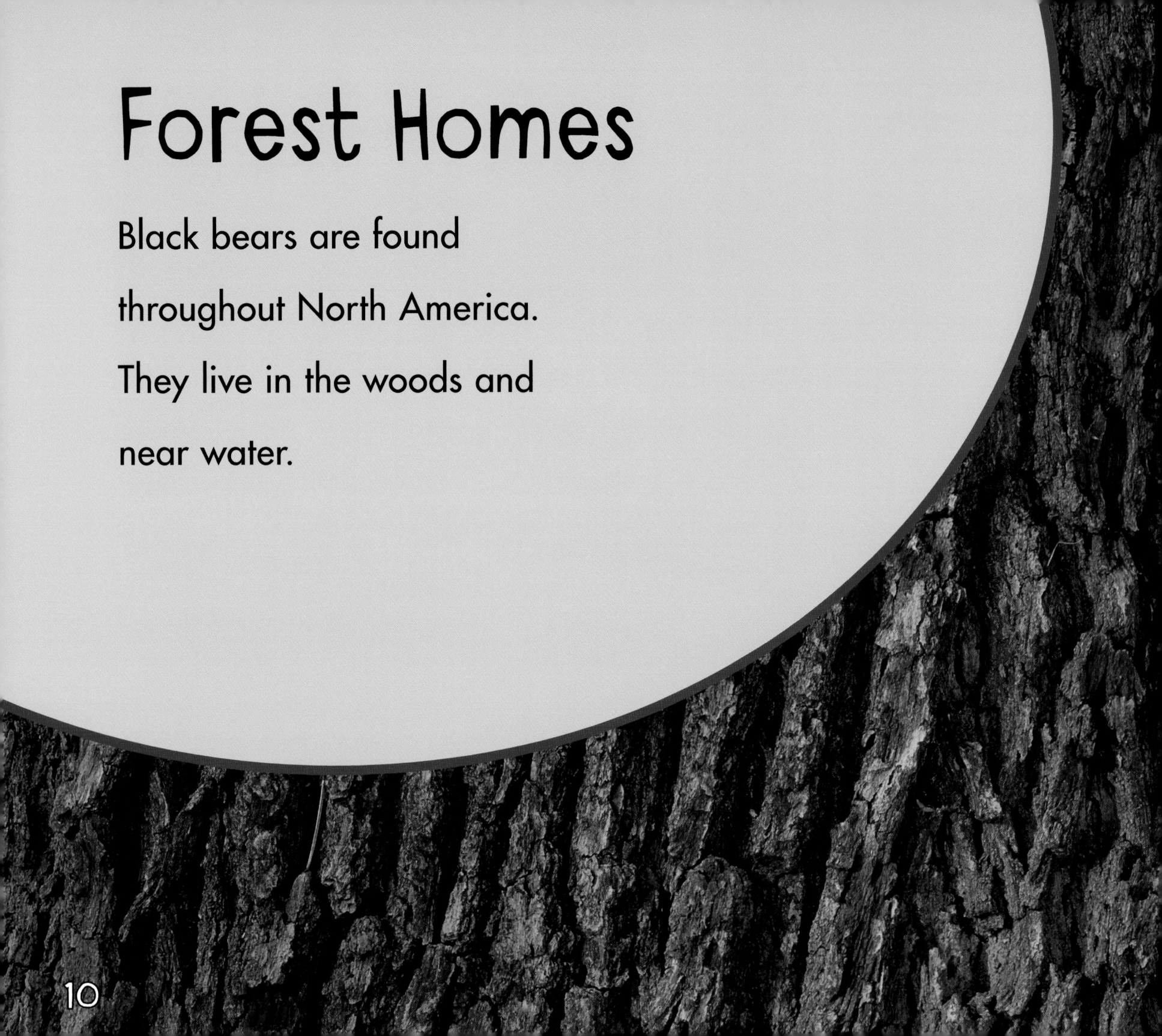

North American Black Bear Range Map

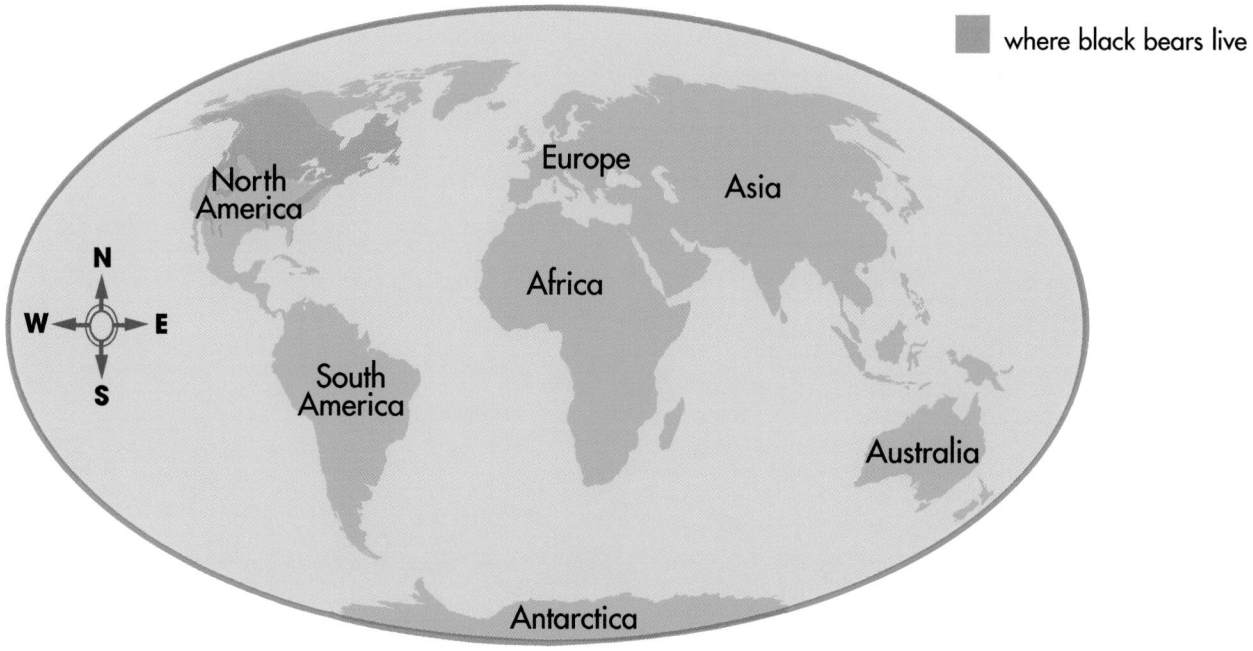

Black bears live in homes called dens. A den can be found in many places. It can be in a cave, a hollow log, or dug into the ground.

Finding Food

Black bears are not picky eaters. They eat berries, bugs, and fish. Black bears sniff with their noses to find food.

Black bears can smell food at campsites. Campers keep their food away from bears. Campers hide their food and pick up their trash.

Life Cycle

A mother black bear gives birth to one to five cubs at a time. Her babies are born covered in fur. The cubs are born blind.

Cubs stay with their mothers
for a year and a half.
Then they leave to live
on their own. Black bears can
live up to 20 years in the wild.

Glossary

blind—unable to see or having very limited sight

cub—a young bear

den—a place where a wild animal may live; a den may be a hole in the ground or a trunk of a tree

fur—thick hair that covers an animal

hollow—empty on the inside

muzzle—an animal's nose, mouth, and jaw

woods—a large area covered with trees and plants; forests are sometimes called woods

Read More

Borgert-Spaniol, Megan. *Black Bears.* North American Animals. Minneapolis: Bellwether Media, 2015.

Kolpin, Molly. *American Black Bears.* Bears. Mankato, Minn.: Capstone Press, 2012.

Magby, Meryl. *Black Bears.* American Animals. New York: PowerKids Press, 2014.

Internet Sites

FactHound offers a safe, fun way to find Internet sites related to this book. All of the sites on FactHound have been researched by our staff.

Here's all you do:

Visit *www.facthound.com*

Type in this code: 9781515708148

Critical Thinking Using the Common Core

1. What helps black bears climb trees? (Key Ideas and Details)
2. What is a den? (Craft and Structure)
3. How long do cubs stay with their mothers? (Key Ideas and Details)

Index

bodies, 6
campers, 16
claws, 4
climbing, 4
cubs, 18, 20
dens, 12
food, 14, 16
fur, 8, 18
habitat, 10
legs, 6
life span, 20
muzzles, 8
noses, 14
paws, 4
weight, 6